# THE

# Gospel

## MADE

## CLEAR

## to Children

**STUDY GUIDE**

Published by
**Free Grace Press**
3900 Dave Ward Dr., Ste. 1900
Conway, AR 72034
(501) 214-9663
email: support@freegracepress.com
website: www.freegracepress.com

Printed in the United States of America

Cover design by Scott Schaller
Front cover illustration copyright ©2022 Elisabeth Adams

ISBN: 978-1-952599-42-2

For additional Reformed Baptist titles, please email us for a free list or see our website at the above address.

# THE *Gospel* MADE CLEAR to Children

>> STUDY GUIDE <<

JENNIFER ADAMS

FREE GRACE PRESS

# STUDY QUESTIONS FOR EXAMINATION AND APPLICATION

We are thankful you have chosen to work through this study guide to *The Gospel Made Clear to Children*. As you work through it, we pray you will consider the holiness of God, the sinful condition of your soul, and the provision God has made for you in His Son, Jesus Christ. He is our only hope and salvation!

Before you begin, we have a few suggestions for how to use the book and study guide:

First, remember to pray before reading each chapter, asking God to give you understanding.

Next, look up the Bible references before answering the study guide questions.

Then, write your answers carefully and thoughtfully. This is the time to let the truth of God's Word do its saving work in your heart.

Finally, ask God to help you apply what you have learned.

We are praying for you!

# *1*

## *High and Holy*
## God's Attributes and Worth

1. Read Isaiah 40:25; 46:9; Deuteronomy 4:39; 2
   Samuel 7:22 ; Jeremiah 10:6–10. Describe God.

   _____

   _____

   _____

   _____

2. How do sinless seraphim respond in the presence
   of a holy God? (Isaiah 6:2)

   _____

   _____

   _____

3. Can sinful men enter the presence of a holy God?
   (1 Timothy 6:15–16)

   _____

   _____

   _____

4. How does a holy God care for the people He has made? (Acts 14:17)

5. What does God rule over? (Psalm 103:19)

6. What kind of ruler is God? (Daniel 2:20; Deuteronomy 32:4; Psalm 31:19; 145:9)

7. What are the four things God cannot do?

8. Where is God? What is He doing there?

_____

_____

_____

9. What is God doing from His throne? (Psalm 11:4–5)

_____

_____

_____

_____

10. What have you learned about God that you did not know before?

_____

_____

_____

_____

> *Dear Lord God, thank You for revealing Yourself through Your Word. You are holy, righteous, and good. Thank You for making me and taking care of me. You are a faithful God. Amen.*

# 2

## *Dwelling in Perfect Delight*
### God the Father, Son, and Spirit

1. For how long has God been God? (Deuteronomy 33:27; Revelation 4:8)

2. What does God depend on for His existence? (Psalm 50:10–12)

3. What does God need to make Him happy? (Acts 17:25)

4.  What was God doing before He made the world?
    (Proverbs 8:22–31)

    _____

    _____

    _____

    _____

5.  How many Gods are there? (Deuteronomy 6:4)

    _____

6.  Who are the three persons in the Trinity?
    (Matthew 28:19)

    _____

    _____

    _____

    _____

7.  What is the role of the Father?

    _____

    _____

    _____

    _____

8. What is the role of the Son?

9. What is the role of the Spirit?

10. Why did God create the world?

11. What is the role of the Father in creation?
    (Hebrews 11:3; Psalm 33:9)

12. What is the role of the Son in creation?
(John 1:3; Colossians 1:16)

13. What is the role of the Spirit in creation?
(Genesis 1:2; Psalm 104:30)

14. What is the role of the Father in salvation?
(Ephesians 1:4–6; John 3:16)

15. What is the role of the Son in salvation?
(Hebrews 10:7; Romans 5:8)

16. What is the role of the Spirit in salvation?
    (John 3:5; 6:63; Titus 3:4–6)

17. Why did God decide to save sinners?
    (John 14:23; Ephesians 1:6; 2:7)

> Dear Lord God, thank You for showing Your glory in creation. Thank You for showing Your love in salvation. Please help me to know You and love You. Amen.

# 3

## *Most Beautiful and Blessed*
### God, the Source of All Happiness

1. Why is heaven described with images of gold, jewels, and delicious fruit?

2. What makes heaven beautiful? (Revelation 4:2–3)

3. How is God to be worshiped? (John 4:24; 2 Corinthians 5:7)

4. Where is God's beauty most clearly seen?
   (2 Corinthians 4:6; John 5:39)

 

5. How do New Testament saints know that
   "God is love"? (1 John 4:10; Romans 5:8)

 

> *Dear Lord God, please help me to see Your Son, by faith, as He is revealed in the Scriptures, that I might worship Him. You alone are worthy. Amen.*

# 4

## *A Place of Judgment*
### God's Throne

1. Why is God worthy of perfect obedience? (Revelation 4:11)

2. What standard does God use to judge men? (James 2:10; Galatians 3:10; John 12:48; Hebrews 4:12)

3. How will sinners be judged? (Romans 2:6; Revelation 20:13; Matthew 12:36)

4. Who is all sin ultimately against?

5. Why is all sin against God?

> Dear Lord God, You are just in all Your judgments and righteous in all Your ways. I have fallen short of Your glory and have disobeyed Your commands. Please help me see myself as I truly am—a sinner in need of a Savior. Amen.

# 5

## Man's Greatest Problem
### God Judges Sinners

1. What is true of every person born into this world?
   (Romans 5:12)

   _____

   _____

   _____

2. Why is sin so terrible?

   _____

   _____

   _____

3. Why is sin our greatest problem?

   _____

   _____

   _____

4. Why is sin our own worst enemy?

5. Describe the condition of a sinner's heart.
   (Ephesians 2:1–3; Jeremiah 17:9; Romans 3:10–11)

6. What is our righteousness to God? (Isaiah 64:6)

7. What is the punishment for sin?
   (Romans 2:5–6; Romans 6:23; Matthew 25:46;
   Galatians 3:10)

> *Dear Lord God, I have no righteousness of my own. I have sinned against You. I have broken Your law. Please help me to repent of my sins and trust in You for salvation. Amen.*

# 6

## A Shocking Provision
### God Sends His Son

1. How can a just and holy God receive sinful rebels as His beloved children?

2. Describe the qualifications of the Savior.

3. Why couldn't God have just created another man, without sin, to be the Savior?

4. Who is the only one qualified to be the Savior of sinners?

_____

_____

_____

5. What did the Son of God do to become the Savior of sinners? (Philippians 2:6–8; John 1:14).

_____

_____

_____

6. Why did the Son agree to this humiliation, suffering, and pain? (Hebrews 10:5–7; 12:1–2)

_____

_____

_____

*Dear Lord God, I praise You for Your wisdom in designing a way to save sinners. I praise You for sending Your Son, the only one who is qualified to save sinners. Please help me to trust in Him. Amen.*

# 7

## *God Made Flesh*
## Jesus the Son of God

1. Who did God send to announce the birth of the Savior? (Luke 2:10)

   _____

   _____

2. What was the sign of the Savior? (Luke 2:10–14)

   _____

   _____

3. Why was Jesus born in Bethlehem? (Micah 5:2)

   _____

   _____

   _____

> *Dear Lord Jesus, I thank You for taking the body the Father prepared for You. I praise You for coming to save sinners. Please help me to put my trust in You. Amen.*

# 8

## *God's Greatest Gift*
### Jesus the King Is Born

1.  When Mary and Joseph presented Jesus in Jerusalem, who recognized Him as the Savior?

2.  What was Simeon's prophecy?

3.  How was the coming of the magi a demonstration of faith?

4. How did the magi express their worship?

_____

_____

_____

_____

> *Dear Lord Jesus, You are the King of Kings. You are the fulfillment of all the Old Testament promises and prophecies. Help me to esteem You as my greatest treasure. Amen.*

# 9

## An Obedient Son
### Jesus's Childhood

1. What was Jesus like as a child?

2. What was the primary characteristic that set Jesus apart from other children?

3. What might Jesus have been discussing with the teachers in the temple during the Passover?

4. What did Jesus mean by the statement, "Did you not know that I had to be in My Father's house?"

_____

_____

_____

_____

5. How might Jesus have prepared in His childhood and young adult years for His calling to be the sin-bearer?

_____

_____

_____

_____

*Dear Lord Jesus, I praise You that You know what it is like to be young. Please help me to walk in love and obedience to the Father, just as You did. Amen.*

# 10

## *Behold the Lamb*
### Jesus's Baptism, Temptation, and Teaching

1. Name two reasons why Jesus was baptized, though He had no sin.

2. Who bore witness to Jesus's deity during His baptism? (Matthew 3:13–17)

3. Name four reasons why the Spirit led Jesus into the wilderness to be tempted.

4. What was the message Jesus began to preach immediately following His temptation? (Matthew 4:17)

5. What is true blessedness? (Matthew 5:3–12)

6. What did Jesus teach about riches? (Matthew 6:16–34)

7. What did Jesus teach about hell? (Matthew 5:27–30; 7:13)

8.  What did Jesus teach about the kingdom of heaven? (Matthew 7:13–23)

9.  What did Jesus teach about prayer? (Matthew 6:5–14; 7:7–12)

10. What did Jesus teach about our attitude toward our enemies? (Matthew 5:21–26, 38–48)

11. How will we know a true Christian from a false one? (Matthew 7:15–23)

12. What will Jesus say to those who think they are Christians but do not do His will? (Matthew 7:21–23)

_____

_____

_____

_____

13. What is one of the main themes of Jesus's parables?

_____

_____

_____

_____

> *Dear Lord Jesus, I praise You for the example You gave in Your baptism. Please create in me a heart to follow You and do all Your holy will. Amen.*

# 11

## *Follow Me*
## Jesus's Call to Discipleship

1. How did Jesus call Peter (Luke 5:1–11), and what did Jesus call Peter to do? (Luke 5:10; Matthew 4:19)

2. How many disciples did Jesus call as apostles? Describe His relationship with them.

3. Did Jesus have other disciples? (Luke 10:1; John 6:54–66)

4. What role did women have in the ministry?
   (Luke 8:1–3; Matthew 27:55; 28:1–10)

   _____

   _____

   _____


5. What did Jesus say would happen to those who
   followed Him? (Matthew 10:16–41)

   _____

   _____

   _____


6. What reward did Jesus promise to those who
   follow Him? (Mark 10:29–30)

   _____

   _____

   _____


> *Dear Lord Jesus, the cost of following You is high, but the price of not following You is unthinkable. You are worthy of every cross and every loss because You are of greater value than anything I might lose. Help me to count You worthy and to follow You in obedience to Your Word. Amen.*

# 12

## *God's Servant*
## Jesus's Wisdom, Power, and Miracles

1. Why did Jesus do miracles? (Acts 2:22; Hebrews 2:4; Matthew 9:35)

2. How was Jesus received by the religious leaders?

3. What did Jesus say to Martha, and what does it mean? (Luke 10:38–42)

4.  Why did Jesus overturn the money-changers'
    tables at the temple? (Matthew 21:12–13; John
    2:13–17)

5.  What did Jesus prophesy would happen to Him?
    (Matthew 16:21; Luke 9:22)

6.  Why did Jesus wait before coming to Mary and
    Martha? (John 11:4)

7. How did Jesus raise Lazarus from the dead? (John 11:43)

_____

_____

_____

8. How was Mary of Bethany's anointing of Jesus an act of faith? (John 12:1–7)

_____

_____

_____

_____

> _Dear Lord Jesus, please help me choose the good part by sitting at Your feet, listening to Your Word. Help me to believe, and please give me new life in You. Amen._

# 13

## *The Final Week*
## Jesus Establishes the New Covenant

1. How did Jesus respond as His suffering drew near? (John 12:27–28)

2. Why did Jesus wash His disciples' feet? (John 13:1–17)

3. Did Jesus know who would betray Him? (John 13:21–27). Why didn't He try to stop him? (John 17:2)

4. Why did Jesus desire to eat the Passover with His disciples?

5. What new commandment did Jesus give when He established the new covenant? (John 13:34)

6. After Peter and the other disciples declared that they were willing to die for the Lord, what did Jesus say they would do? (Matthew 26:31–35)

7. What were some of Jesus's final instructions? (John 14–16)

8. What did Jesus pray for His disciples? (John 17)

*Dear Lord Jesus, please help me to recognize my sin and my need for salvation. Please wash me in Your blood and grant me forgiveness of sins through Your finished work on the cross. Amen.*

# 14

## *Thy Will Be Done*
## Jesus Submits to the Cross

1. When Jesus was praying in the garden and the weight of sin was placed upon Him, how did He respond? (Luke 22:39–46; Matthew 26:36–46)

2. What was the cup from which Jesus drank? (Matthew 26:39, 42; Jeremiah 25:15–17; Psalm 75:7–8; Job 21:20; Isaiah 51:17)

3. Since Jesus drank the cup of the Father's wrath, what cup do those who put their trust in Him drink? (1 Corinthians 10:16)

4. How did Judas betray the Lord? (Luke 22:47–48)

5. What did Jesus's disciples do when He was arrested? (Matthew 26:56)

6. Did Jesus admit to being the Son of God?
   (Luke 22:70)


7. How did the religious leaders respond when Jesus
   said that He is the Son of God? (Matthew 26:65)


8. Why did they accuse Him of blasphemy?


9. Did Jesus admit to being the King of the Jews?
   (Luke 23:3)

10. What was Pilate's verdict regarding Jesus?
    (Luke 23:14)

11. Though Pilate knew Jesus was innocent, what did
    he decide to do with Jesus and why?
    (Mark 15:15; John 19:12–13)

12. What happened to the robber and murderer
    named Barabbas, and who does he picture?
    (Luke 23:25)

13. Men said to Jesus, "If You are the Son of God, come down from the cross" (Matthew 27:40). He is the Son of God, so why did He stay on the cross?

_Dear Lord Jesus, thank You for drinking the Father's cup of wrath so that those who trust in You can drink the Father's cup of blessing. Please help me to trust in You. Amen._

# 15

## *In the Place of Sinners*
## Jesus's Suffering and Death

1. What did Jesus promise the repentant robber on the cross, and how could He do that? (Luke 23:43)

2. When Jesus was on the cross, what happened to the relationship between Him and the Father?

3. Why did Jesus submit to the cross? (Hebrews 2:10; 10:7; 12:2; Isaiah 53:10–12; Philippians 2:8–11)

4. What happened at three o'clock in the afternoon, and what does it mean? (John 19:30; Luke 23:44–47)

5. How could God's wrath against a multitude of sinners be removed by the death of one man?

6. Why do sinners need to be credited with Jesus's righteousness?

7. What was necessary to bring sinners near to the Father?

8. What was done to confirm Jesus's death? (John 19:31–37)

9. Where was Jesus buried? (Matthew 27:57–61)

10. Who did Pilate send to guard the tomb and why? (Matthew 27:62–66)

## 11. What did the women plan to do? (Luke 23:54–56)

_____

_____

_____

_____

*Dear Lord God, please help me understand what happened on the cross and what it means for those who repent of their sins and trust in You. Amen.*

# 16

## *Mission Accomplished!*
### Jesus's Resurrection

1.  When did Jesus rise from the dead? (Matthew 28:1–6)

    _____

    _____

    _____

2.  How do we know Jesus rose from the dead? (Matthew 28:2–7)

    _____

    _____

    _____

3.  Who raised Jesus from the dead? (Acts 2:24; Romans 8:11; John 2:19–21; 10:17–18)

    _____

    _____

    _____

4. What did God declare by the resurrection of Jesus? (Romans 1:4)

_____

_____

_____

_____

5. What does the resurrection prove concerning Jesus's offering of Himself in the place of sinners?

_____

_____

_____

_____

6. To what does the resurrection testify?

_____

_____

_____

_____

7. What did the angel tell the women?
   (Luke 24:1–11; Mark 16:1–8; Matthew 28:1–8)

8. Why didn't Mary Magdalene recognize Jesus at first?

9. When did the two men on the road to Emmaus recognize Jesus? (Luke 24:30–31)

10. Why did Jesus ask the disciples if they had something to eat?

11. What did Thomas say when he put his finger in Jesus's hands and side? (John 20:27–28)

_____

_____

_____

_____

*Dear Lord Jesus, I praise You for Your resurrection and how it proves the Father's acceptance of Your sacrifice in the place of sinners. Please open my eyes to see You as the crucified and risen Savior. Amen.*

# 17

## *Witnesses to His Resurrection*
## Jesus Gives the Great Commission

1. To whom did Jesus appear after His resurrection?
   (1 Corinthians 15:3–7; John 20:16–18; Matthew
   28:1–10)

   _____

   _____

   _____

   _____

   _____

2. Why did Jesus ask Peter three times if he loved
   Him?

   _____

   _____

   _____

   _____

   _____

3. What did Jesus command the disciples to wait for? (Acts 1:4–5)

_____

_____

_____

_____

4. What did Jesus commission the disciples to do? (Matthew 28:18–20)

_____

_____

_____

_____

5. What is the primary message Jesus gave His disciples to teach? (Acts 2:22–24, 32, 37–39)

_____

_____

_____

_____

_____

6. Where did Jesus go when He ascended into the cloud? (Acts 1:9–11)

7. What did the disciples do after Jesus's ascension? (Acts 1:12–14)

# 18

## The Ascended King
## Jesus's Coronation and Exaltation

1. Why is the heavenly exaltation of Jesus Christ so amazing since He is God and was exalted as God before the creation of the world?

2. What is Jesus doing now as He is seated at the Father's right hand? (Hebrews 7:25)

3. To what does Jesus Christ's heavenly exaltation testify?

4. What was Jesus's first official act as risen and exalted King? (Acts 2:1–4)

5. Name at least four things the Holy Spirit does for the believer.

6. Name at least four things Jesus Christ is doing now from His throne.

_____

_____

_____

_____

_____

*Dear Lord Jesus, You are the ascended and exalted King of Kings! I praise You for the victory You accomplished by Your heavenly exaltation. Please add me to Your heavenly train of followers. Amen.*

# 19

## Bow Before the King
### Repent and Believe

1. When the disciples were filled with the Spirit, what did they do? (Acts 2:11)

2. When Peter was filled with the Spirit, what did he say before the crowd? (Acts 2:22–24)

3. What did Peter call the people of Jerusalem to do? (Acts 2:38)

_____

_____

_____

4. What is the same Holy Spirit calling you to do?

_____

_____

5. What does it mean to repent?

_____

_____

_____

6. What is the heart's desire of a truly repentant person?

_____

_____

_____

7. Fill in the blanks. Repentance is turning away from _____ and turning to _____.

8. What does "repentance is not a one-time action—it is a way of life" mean?

_____

_____

_____

9. What is repentance a sign of?

_____

_____

_____

10. Does repentance mean we never sin? If not, what does it mean?

_____

_____

_____

_____

*Dear Lord God, please show me my sins. Please help me confess and forsake my sins. Please help me believe in Jesus alone for salvation. Amen.*

# *20*

## *Trust the King*
### Confess and Believe

1. What does it mean to believe?

   _____

   _____

   _____

   _____

2. What is faith?

   _____

   _____

   _____

   _____

3. What does the Bible promise concerning salvation? (Acts 16:31)

   _____

   _____

   _____

4. What does it mean to believe in Jesus?

5. What does it mean to rely on Christ's work for us?

6. Can a person be made right with God by his own good behavior?

7. What does it mean to trust in Christ's death for us?

8. What does God promise to those who confess and forsake their sins? (1 John 1:9; Proverbs 28:13)

9. What does "believing in Jesus is not a one-time decision—it is a life-time commitment" mean?

10. What is the proof of someone who believes in Jesus?

*Dear Lord God, please help me to look to Jesus alone for salvation. Please help me to believe in Him. Please make me one of Your children in Christ. Amen.*

# *21*

## *Kiss the King*
## Judgment Is Coming

1. What will Jesus do when He returns as King of Kings and Lord of Lords? (Acts 10:42; 2 Timothy 4:1)

2. Who will be judged? (Acts 10:42)

3. What will Jesus use to judge everyone? (John 12:48; Revelation 19:11–16)

4. What will they be judged for? (Romans 2:5–6; 2 Thessalonians 1:7–10)

5. What will happen to the guilty? (Matthew 25:46)

6. Who will be saved from judgment? (Acts 16:31; Romans 5:9)

7. What is the reward for those who will be saved? (John 3:15–16; 2 Peter 3:13)

8. Why do we struggle to believe that God will judge us for our sins?

9.  When will we be judged?

10. What must we do to be saved from judgment?

11. Who is your only refuge and salvation?

12. Will you repent of your sins and trust in Jesus?

> *Dear Lord God, please open my eyes to see Your holiness and to recognize my sinfulness. Please help me to repent of my sins and to trust in Jesus alone for salvation. Amen.*

# 22

## *New Heart*
## A Changed Relationship with God

1. Do you recognize that you are a sinner?

2. Do you agree that God would be just to punish you for your sins?

3. Are you willing to give up self-righteousness?

4. Will you place all your hope in the life, death, and resurrection of Jesus Christ to be made right with God?

5. What happens to someone who truly repents and believes in Jesus?

6. How is a person's relationship with God changed when they believe?

7. What is the believer's attitude toward the Bible?

8. What is the believer's attitude toward God's commands?

9. What is the believer's attitude toward prayer?

10. What is the role of persecution in the believer's life?

11. What might a believer suffer for the sake of Christ?

12. Why is a believer willing to suffer for the sake of Christ?

_____

_____

_____

_____

13. What is the believer's greatest concern?

_____

_____

_____

_____

> _Dear Lord God, please make me a new person in Christ. Please give me a heart to seek You in Your Word and in prayer. Please help me to desire You above all things. Amen._

# 23

## New Life
## A Changed Relationship with Sin

1. How is a person's relationship with sin changed when they believe? (Romans 6:11)

2. What does a believer do when they sin? (2 Corinthians 7:10; 1 John 1:9–10; 2:1–2)

3. What is the believer's attitude toward sin?

4. What is the role of the Holy Spirit in the believer? (Romans 8:13–16)

5. What is the believer's relationship to this world? (1 John 2:15–17)

6. Where is the believer's true citizenship and hope? (Philippians 3:20; Colossians 3:1–4)

*Dear Lord God, please help me to confess my sins and forsake them. Please cleanse me and make me new. Please help me to turn away from the world to follow You. Amen.*

# 24

## *New Mission*

# A Changed Relationship with Others

1. How is a person's relationship with other Christians changed when they believe? (John 13:35; 1 John 3:14)

2. What is the proof of being Jesus's disciple? (John 13:35)

3. How are believers to love one another? (1 John 3:16)

4. What is meant by the term "fellowship"?
   (Philippians 1:27)

   _____

   _____

   _____


5. What is the believer's attitude toward those who
   do not know Christ?

   _____

   _____

   _____


6. What is the believer's attitude toward the spread
   of the gospel and missions?

   _____

   _____

   _____


7. What is the believer's attitude toward eternity?

   _____

   _____

   _____

8. How does a believer live in light of eternity?

_____

_____

_____

_____

9. Will you give yourself more fully to the Word of God and to prayer?

_____

_____

_____

_____

*Dear Lord God, please help me to deny myself, take up my cross, and follow You. Please help me to tell others the good news of Jesus Christ and all He has done to save sinners. Amen.*